THE LOTTERY WINNER

Just think. You win five million pounds in the lottery – suddenly you are rich! What are you going to do with all that money? You can buy clothes, cars, houses; you can go to New York, London, Moscow, Paris, Madrid . . .

Jason Williams is a very happy young man. He has a winning lottery ticket – and a cheque for five million pounds. But other people want his money too. His mother, his father, his wife, and his lawyer. Jason is in trouble with the police. He needs a lawyer's help, and lawyers are expensive. And then there's Emma Carter.

Emma Carter is very angry and unhappy. She says that it is *her* ticket, and that *she* won the lottery, not Jason Williams. Emma Carter has a lawyer too, because she wants her five million pounds, and she wants it now.

So who's going to get the money? Where did Jason get the winning lottery ticket from? Who is telling the truth – and who is telling lies?

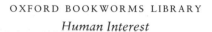

OXFORD BOOKWORMS LIBRARY

Human Interest

The Lottery Winner

Stage 1 (400 headwords)

Series Editor: Jennifer Bassett
Founder Editor: Tricia Hedge
Activities Editors: Jennifer Bassett and Alison Baxter

ROSEMARY BORDER

The Lottery Winner

OXFORD UNIVERSITY PRESS

OXFORD

UNIVERSITY PRESS

Great Clarendon Street, Oxford OX2 6DP

Oxford University Press is a department of the University of Oxford.
It furthers the University's objective of excellence in research, scholarship,
and education by publishing worldwide in

Oxford New York

Auckland Cape Town Dar es Salaam Hong Kong Karachi
Kuala Lumpur Madrid Melbourne Mexico City Nairobi
New Delhi Shanghai Taipei Toronto

With offices in

Argentina Austria Brazil Chile Czech Republic France Greece
Guatemala Hungary Italy Japan Poland Portugal Singapore
South Korea Switzerland Thailand Turkey Ukraine Vietnam

OXFORD and OXFORD ENGLISH are registered trade marks of
Oxford University Press in the UK and in certain other countries

ISBN 978 0 19 478907 3

A complete recording of this Bookworms edition of
The Lottery Winner is available on audio CD ISBN 978 0 19 478842 7

Printed in China

ACKNOWLEDGEMENTS
Illustrated by: David Lloyd

Word count (main text): 5655 words

For more information on the Oxford Bookworms Library,
visit www.oup.com/bookworms

CONTENTS

Chapter 1
The bag-snatcher

One Saturday afternoon in a small town, Emma Carter came out of a shoe shop with some new shoes. They were cheap shoes, but Emma was very pleased with them. She was seventy-three years old and did not have much money. She began to walk home. 'A nice cup of tea,' she thought, 'and then I can go for a walk in my new shoes.'

It was a quiet town and there was nobody in the street. Suddenly, Emma heard something behind her. She did not have time to look, because just then somebody ran up behind her, hit her on the head, and snatched her bag out of her hands. Emma fell down on her back. Then she looked up, and saw a tall young man with long, dirty brown hair. He stood and looked down at her for a second; then he ran away with Emma's bag under his arm.

'Help! Help!' Emma cried.

But nobody came, and after two or three minutes Emma slowly got up and went to the nearest house. The people there were very kind. They gave Emma a cup of tea, and soon an ambulance came and took her to hospital.

At the hospital a doctor looked at Emma's head and back. 'You're going to be OK,' he said. 'Just take it easy for a day or two. Can your husband help you at home?'

'My husband died eight years ago,' said Emma. 'There's only me at home.'

'Well,' the doctor said, 'we don't want you to feel ill and fall downstairs at home. So I think you must stay in

He ran away with Emma's bag under his arm.

2

hospital for tonight, and perhaps tomorrow night, too.'
Later, a policeman came to the hospital and Emma told
him about the bag-snatcher.

'Did anybody see this young man?' he asked.

'I don't know,' said Emma. 'But there was nobody in
the street when I called for help.'

'Oh dear,' the policeman said. 'What was in your bag?'

'A little money – and a lottery ticket,' said Emma. 'I
buy a ticket every Saturday. Then on Saturday evening I
watch the lottery on television. I always have the same
numbers – 5, 12, 23, 24, 38, 41. All those numbers are
important to me. I was born on 5th December, 1923. I lived
at number 24 Sandwich Road for 38 years . . .'

'Yes, yes,' said the policeman. 'I understand.' He wrote
everything down in a little black book. 'Did you see the
man's face?' he asked.

'Yes,' said Emma. 'I did. I fell on my back, and he looked
down at me for a second. So I saw his face.'

The policeman opened a small bag. In it there were a
lot of pictures of eyes and ears, hair and mouths. 'I need a
picture of the man's face. Can you help me?' he said.

'Yes,' said Emma. 'He was tall and he had long, dirty
brown hair. He wore blue trousers and a white shirt with
a picture of a footballer. He had brown eyes . . .' Carefully
she took the small pictures and made a big picture of the
young man's face. She checked the picture carefully.

Emma made a picture of the young man's face.

'What colour were his shoes?' asked the policeman.

Shoes! Suddenly Emma remembered her new shoes. Where were they? She told the policeman about her shoes, but then she began to cry and could not stop.

A nurse came up to Emma's bed. 'Please go now,' she said to the policeman. 'Mrs Carter needs to sleep.'

Chapter 2

The winning ticket

Jason Williams came home and sat down on his bed. He was twenty-two years old. He lived with his father and mother in three small rooms at the top of a tall building. Every day he went out, but he did not go to work. Jason stole things. Sometimes he stole things from shops or cars; and sometimes he stole money from old people like Emma Carter. Today he was angry.

'I took that old woman's bag,' he thought. 'What did I get? Two pounds, seventy-four pence, and a lottery ticket!

'Two pounds, seventy-four pence, and a lottery ticket!'

And it was an old, cheap bag too.'

Jason knew about lottery tickets. He bought five tickets every weekend. He put Emma's lottery ticket in his pocket and forgot about it. Then he went out for a drink.

At the hospital a nurse put Emma to bed in a room with five other women. There was a television in the room, and at eight o'clock everybody watched the lottery. For a minute Emma watched too, but she felt very tired and soon she closed her eyes and slept. So she did not hear the winning numbers for that week's lottery . . .

On Sunday at twelve o'clock Jason got out of bed and made some tea. Then he opened his father's newspaper and found the winning lottery numbers: 5, 12, 23, 24, 38, 41. He checked his five lottery tickets. 'No good!' he said.

Then he remembered the old woman's ticket and checked those numbers too: 5, 12, 23, 24, 38, 41. He checked them three times. Six winning numbers!

'I'm a winner!' he said. He kissed the ticket. Then he ran into the living-room and kissed his mother.

'Here, what's the matter, Jason?' said Lily Williams. Jason sometimes hit her, but he did not usually kiss her. Her cigarette fell out of her mouth.

'I'm this week's winner, Mum! I'm rich!'

'The lottery! I'm this week's winner, Mum! Look – six winning numbers. I'm rich!'

Jason's father came into the living-room. 'What's all this noise?' he said.

'Joe, Joe!' said Lily. 'Jason's got six winning numbers in the lottery. We're rich!'

'Wrong!' said Jason. *'I'm* rich.'

7

His mother and father began to speak at the same time. But Jason did not listen. He went out to the telephone box in the street and made a very important telephone call.

On Monday morning a policeman came to the hospital with Emma's new shoes.

'A little girl found them in the street and took them to the police station,' he said.

'How kind of her!' said Emma.

'We found your bag too,' said the policeman. 'But there's nothing in it, Mrs Carter. I'm sorry.'

'It doesn't matter,' said Emma. 'I'm very pleased to have the bag. My son gave it to me a long time ago. He lives in Australia, but he telephones me every week . . . And now I've got my new shoes too. Thank you very much.' Suddenly she felt happier.

That evening an ambulance took Emma home. She made a cup of tea and sat down to watch the television news.

The newsreader smiled into Emma's living-room.

'And now for this week's lottery winner. The winning numbers were: 5, 12, 23, 24, 38, 41. And here is the man with the winning ticket – Jason

*Williams! Jason is twenty-two and now he's a
rich man. He's got a cheque from Sunshine
Lotteries for five million pounds. That's a lot of
money! Well, Jason, how are you feeling
tonight?'*
'Wonderful!'
'And what are you going to do with your money?
'Oh, I'm going to buy a house with fifty rooms,
and a big expensive car. I'm going to go to New
York, Miami . . .'*

Emma looked at the young man on the television. Jason
Williams had a big smile on his face, but he had long, dirty
brown hair, brown eyes . . . Emma sat up quickly. 'That's
the man!' she thought. 'I remember his face. He hit me
and snatched my bag, and stole my lottery ticket – *my*
winning ticket, with *my* winning numbers!'

She got up and went to the telephone. 'Hullo – police?'
she said.

Chapter 3

Jason in trouble

At ten o'clock on Monday night Jason was a very happy man. He was in a big room in a hotel with a lot of people in beautiful clothes. There were television cameras, reporters, people from Sunshine Lotteries . . . Everybody had a drink in their hands, and a girl went round the room with a bottle of champagne.

'Hullo!' said Jason. 'Come in and have some champagne!'

'Have some more champagne,' she said to Jason.

Jason's face went very red. He snatched the bottle and took a long drink. The champagne ran down his new blue shirt. He laughed. 'Kiss me,' he said to the girl.

Suddenly the door opened and two men came in.

'Hullo!' said Jason. 'Come in and have some champagne! It's OK – Sunshine Lotteries are paying for it!'

But the two men were not interested in champagne. They were policemen. Everybody stopped talking and looked at them.

'Is Jason Williams here?' one of the policemen said.

'That's me,' said Jason. 'What do you want?'

'We'd like to ask you some questions, Mr Williams. At the police station. Come with us, please.'

⑤ ⑫ ㉓ ㉔ ㊳ ㊶

On Tuesday morning Jason was tired and unhappy. He was in a small room at the police station, and there were two policemen in the room with him. One policeman stood by the door, and watched and listened. The second policeman sat at a table and asked questions, questions, questions – the same questions, again and again.

'Now,' said the policeman. 'Tell me again. Where were you at four o'clock on Saturday afternoon?'

'At home,' said Jason. 'I'm telling you the truth. Ask my mother and father! I didn't steal anything!'

'I'm not interested in your mother and father,' said the policeman. 'I can talk to them later. At the moment I'm interested in *you*, and your answers to my questions. You were in town on Saturday afternoon. We know that, because a woman saw you.'

'No!' said Jason. 'That's a lie. I was at home all afternoon and evening. I watched football on television.'

'Tell me about the football, then. Who won?'

Jason said nothing. His hands and his face felt hot.

'When did the football finish? Five o'clock? Six o'clock?'

'Yes. No,' said Jason. 'I don't remember.'

The policeman smiled. 'How much money was there in the bag, Jason?'

'There wasn't—' Jason stopped. *Careful*, he thought. *Be careful*. 'There wasn't a bag,' he said. 'I told you. I didn't steal the old woman's bag!'

'Old woman? Who said anything about an old woman?' Now Jason felt cold. 'You did,' he said.

'Oh no, I didn't,' said the policeman. 'I talked about a woman. So how did you know she was an *old* woman?'

He stood up. 'Jason Williams, on Saturday afternoon you hit Mrs Emma Carter on the head and snatched her bag. You stole her money and her lottery ticket. Her *winning* lottery ticket – so you stole five million pounds from Mrs Carter. You're in trouble, Williams. Big trouble.'

'I want to see my lawyer,' said Jason suddenly. Jason did not know any lawyers. But people on television always said that.

That afternoon a different policeman took Jason to court. The court was in a big grey building in the middle of the town. Jason and the policeman waited in a small room. The policeman did not look at Jason, and he did not say anything. Jason felt very unhappy.

Then a woman came into the room. She was young, with short brown hair and an interesting face. She wore a

'You're in trouble, Williams. Big trouble.'

black skirt and a white shirt, and carried a big black bag.

'Mr Williams?' she said to Jason. 'I'm Sally Cash, and I'm your lawyer.'

The policeman left the room, and Sally Cash sat down and began to ask Jason questions.

14

Soon a man in a black coat came into the room. 'Are you ready to go into court, Miss Cash?' he asked.

'Nearly ready, John,' said the lawyer. She looked at Jason. 'I'm going to do all the talking in court. OK? I don't want you to say anything. Nothing important is going to happen today. They're going to send you to the Crown Court. That's a more important court.'

'When?' asked Jason.

'Soon.'

'Can I go home tonight?' asked Jason. 'Last night I slept in a cell at the police station. It wasn't very nice.'

'No, I'm sorry,' said Miss Cash. 'You can't go home. You see, you're a rich man now. You can buy a ticket to New York, Hong Kong – you can buy an aeroplane! The police want you to stay in this country.'

'But I want to go home!'

'I can ask the court,' said Sally Cash.

Two men and a woman sat at the end of a long table and listened carefully to everyone's story.

Then the woman looked at Sally Cash. 'This case must go to the Crown Court,' she said. 'Jason Williams must stay at the police station and—'

'Excuse me,' said Sally Cash. 'Mr Williams slept in a police cell last night. He's very young and he was unhappy and afraid. He'd like to go home tonight – please.'

The woman talked quietly to the two men for a minute. Then she said, 'Mr Williams, you can go home tonight. But you must leave your lottery cheque here in court.'

'Why?' asked Jason.

'We don't want you to run away, Mr Williams. Now listen carefully. You must live at your parents' house. Don't leave the town. And every morning at ten o'clock you must go to the police station. Do you understand?'

'Yes,' said Jason.

Chapter 4

Everybody loves a winner

When Jason got home, his mother was very excited. 'We saw you on the news last night,' she said. 'With your cheque for five million pounds. You're rich and famous!'

'I'm in trouble, Mum,' said Jason. 'Please phone the police. Say, "My son was at home on Saturday afternoon. He watched the football on television." Please.'

'I can't say that,' said his mother. 'It isn't true.'

'Would you like ten thousand pounds?' asked Jason suddenly.

'No,' said Lily Williams. 'I always tell the truth.'

'Twenty thousand,' said Jason.

'Why do you want me to tell a lie to the police?' asked Lily. 'What did you do on Saturday afternoon?' She looked at Jason. 'You did something bad. Is that it? And now you want me to tell a lie for you. But I don't tell lies.'

'Thirty thousand!' said Jason. 'Please, Mum! Help me! I slept in a police cell last night, and I was in court this afternoon. Now they're going to send me to the Crown Court. Mum – thirty thousand pounds! Think about it.'

'OK, son,' said Lily Williams slowly. 'For thirty

'*For thirty thousand pounds, I think I can tell a lie,*' *said Lily.*

thousand pounds, I think I can tell a lie. But what did you do on Saturday afternoon? Tell me.'

'Nothing,' said Jason. 'I didn't do anything.'

'So why are they sending you to the Crown Court?'

Jason didn't answer, and his mother looked at him. 'And what about your Dad? He was at home on Saturday afternoon. You weren't, and he knows that. What do you want *him* to say to the police?'

'OK, OK,' said Jason. 'Dad can have thirty thousand pounds too. But not today. My lottery cheque is at the court, and I've only got £2 in my pocket!'

Jason did not sleep well that night. On Wednesday morning at ten o'clock he went to the police station.

'I'm here,' he said.

'You've got a visitor,' said the policeman. 'It's your wife. She wants to see you.'

Jason's mouth opened. 'My wife?' he said. 'But . . .'

The policeman opened a door and called, 'He's here, Mrs Williams!'

A young woman came into the room. 'Hullo, Jason.'

Fiona Williams was small and fat. She had long yellow hair and a big red mouth. She looked at Jason, but she talked to the policeman.

'Jason is my husband,' she said. 'Our son was born two years ago. His name's Jack. I loved Jason, but he wasn't very nice to me. Sometimes he hit me. One night he broke two of my teeth. Then the baby was ill and cried a lot. Jason hit him too. Jack was only two months old, and Jason hit him – a little baby!'

'That's a lie!' said Jason. 'I didn't—'

'Oh yes, you did!' Fiona said. She spoke to the policeman again. 'So I left him, and took the baby with me. Jason didn't look for us. He didn't want us, and he never gave me any money for our son. He went home to his mother and father, and he forgot about little Jack and me. I forgot about Jason too. Then I saw him on television, with a cheque from Sunshine Lotteries for five million pounds. Well, I'm his wife, Jack's his son – and we want half of his money!'

'Well, Mr Williams,' said the policeman. 'Is this woman your wife?'

'Don't ask him, ask me!' Fiona said. 'He's my husband, and I can prove it. I'm going to get a good lawyer, and I'm going to get that two and a half million pounds!'

'Everybody wants my money!' said Jason. 'I'm going to see my lawyer!'

So on Wednesday afternoon Jason went to Sally Cash's office. It was in a big building with 'Evans, Robinson, Dennis and Day' over the door.

'Why isn't your name there too?' asked Jason.

'Because I'm young and not very important,' said Sally with a smile. 'I work for Mr Dennis.'

'*Jason hit him – a little baby!*'

Sally's office was very small. There were books on the table and on all the chairs. Sally moved the books off one chair, and Jason sat down.

'So, Jason,' Sally said, 'you have a wife and son.'

'How do you know that?' said Jason.

'Your wife's lawyer telephoned me this afternoon,' said Sally. 'Your wife wants some of your lottery money. And because she's your wife, and has a two-year-old son, she can get it easily.'

'I'm not going to give her anything,' Jason said. 'She left me. She went away with a new lover, and she took our baby with her. She never wrote or telephoned. I looked for her, but I couldn't find her. I cried every night . . .'

'Your wife tells a different story. She left you because you hit her, and the baby. Is that true?'

'I don't remember,' Jason said angrily. 'It was a long time ago. She just wants my money. Everybody wants my money! But it was *my* lottery ticket, so it's *my* money!'

'Mmm,' said Sally. 'Perhaps it was Mrs Emma Carter's lottery ticket. She remembered the numbers because they were important to her.'

'Huh,' said Jason. 'That old woman just wants my money because she saw me on television. She thought of a good story about the numbers, and now she says that it was her ticket. Did the ticket have her name on it?'

'No. There are no names on lottery tickets.'

'So she can't *prove* that it was her ticket,' said Jason. 'She can't take my money away from me.'

'Perhaps she can, and perhaps she can't. We don't know. But she's going to need a good lawyer. And lawyers are expensive. It isn't going to be easy for her.'

'So that old woman wants *all* the money. Fiona wants *half* of it. My Mum wants thirty thousand pounds, my Dad wants thirty thousand pounds . . .'

'You're forgetting me,' said Sally.

'I don't understand,' Jason said.

'I told you. Lawyers are expensive. And I'm doing a lot of work for you. You can't pay me now, because your cheque is at the court. But I can wait.'

'Oh, thanks very much,' said Jason. 'Very kind of you.'

Sally smiled. 'Now, let's talk about the bag-snatching.'

'I didn't do it.'

Sally looked tired. 'Jason, I want to help you, but it's very difficult. Mrs Carter saw your face in the street, and then she saw you on television. She's going to stand up in the court and say, "That's the man! He stole my bag, my money, and my lottery ticket."'

'But it isn't true,' said Jason. 'I was at home. I watched the football on television. Ask my Mum!'

'How much money are you giving her, Jason?' Sally asked quietly. 'Thirty thousands pounds, was it?'

Jason's face went red. He wanted to hit Sally. She looked

23

Sally looked at his red, angry face, and waited.

at his red, angry face, and waited. Then she said:

'Jason, in the Crown Court a lot of people are going to look at you. They're going to think, "This is a nasty young man. He hits people – his wife, his baby, old women in the street. He steals things. He wins five million pounds in the lottery, but he doesn't want to give a penny to his wife and son. And he tells lies." They're not going to like you, Jason. And that's not going to help you. So, *please*, tell the truth. Say that you're sorry. You're young. You can begin again, stay out of trouble. But you *must* tell the truth to the court.'

Jason thought for a minute. Then he looked at Sally. 'OK,' he said slowly, 'perhaps I took the old woman's bag. But that lottery ticket *wasn't* in her bag. It's *my* ticket. *I* bought it, *I* paid for it, with *my* money. OK?'

Sally Cash did not answer. She looked at Jason for two or three long minutes. Then she said slowly, 'OK, Jason. You stole the bag, but it was your lottery ticket.'

Chapter 5

Emma gets a lawyer

On Wednesday evening Simon Carter telephoned his mother. He lived near Sydney with his wife and their two children, and he telephoned Emma every week. She told him the story of her lottery ticket. Simon listened carefully, and got angrier and angrier.

'Is your head OK now, Mum?'

'Yes, thank you, Simon. But I'm very, very angry. That young man stole my lottery ticket. Now he's got a cheque for five million pounds – and I've got nothing! I don't want to be rich, but I *do* want to come to Australia and visit you, and Mollie, and my grandchildren. It's not right, Simon! I had the winning ticket, I paid for it, and that man stole it!' She began to cry.

'Mum, listen,' said Simon. 'Go and see a lawyer.'

'I don't know any lawyers,' said Emma unhappily.

'Look in the telephone book,' said Simon. 'There are lawyers in every town.'

'But lawyers are expensive. I can't pay a lawyer.'

'*I* can pay a lawyer,' said Simon. 'I'm sending you some money today, through my bank. Don't cry, Mum. Put on your best dress and go and see a lawyer.'

'Simon, you're a wonderful son.'

'And you're a wonderful mother. Goodbye, Mum. And good luck!'

'Well, Mrs Carter, how can I help you?'

It was Thursday morning and Emma was in Edwin Jones's office. Edwin Jones was a big man, with a red face and small blue eyes.

'It's about a lottery ticket,' Emma began.

'Ah, the lottery. Everybody wants to win the lottery!'

'But I *did*!' said Emma. 'It was *my* ticket – *my* numbers.'

'Tell me about it, Mrs Carter. From the beginning.'

So Emma told the lawyer everything, and he listened carefully. When Emma finished, he said:

'Those numbers on the ticket – tell them to me again.'

'5, 12, 23, 24, 38, 41.'

'And you always get a ticket with those numbers. Why, Mrs Carter?' asked the lawyer.

'All those numbers are important to me. I was born on 5th December, 1923. I lived at number 24 Sandwich Road for 38 years. And my son Simon is 41 years old.'

'I see. Well, Mrs Carter,' Mr Jones said. 'What do you want me to do?'

'Please talk to Sunshine Lotteries, Mr Jones. They've got my ticket.'

27

Emma told the lawyer everything.

'But, Mrs Carter, what can they do? All lottery tickets look the same. People don't write their names on their tickets . . . Perhaps it *is* your ticket, but we can't *prove* it.'

'But we can! My ticket's different! Please listen! I always put a little kiss on my ticket . . . you know, an X.'

'Why do you do that?'

'My son lives in Australia with his family. I'd like to visit them, but aeroplane tickets are very expensive. So every week I get a lottery ticket and I think about Simon and his wife and my grandchildren, and I send them a kiss. Simon's a wonderful son. He telephones me every week. He never forgets . . .'

The lawyer smiled. 'Yes, yes, I understand,' he said. 'My mother lives in Wales, and I telephone her every week too. Please go home now, Mrs Carter. I'm going to make some telephone calls. Come and see me again tomorrow.'

Chapter 6

The money and the ticket

Jason did not sleep on Wednesday night. On Thursday morning he got up very early, and made some tea.

'What am I going to do?' he thought. 'They're going to send me to prison because I stole that old woman's bag. But I'm going to say sorry – sorry to the court, sorry to the old woman, sorry to everybody. Then perhaps I can get out of prison after – what did my lawyer say? – only eighteen months. OK. So I go to prison . . . but I don't want

'So I go to prison ...'

to lose that five million pounds! I want the court to believe
it was *my* ticket.'

He drank his tea, and remembered his meeting with Sally
Cash. *They're not going to like you, Jason. They're going
to think, 'This is a nasty young man.'*

'OK,' Jason thought. 'I'm going to do something nice.
What can I do? Yes, I know! Give some of the money away!
I can give it to that charity, "Help the Children". They
send doctors and nurses to Africa and India. I saw them
on television last Christmas. They always need money.
Wonderful! People can't say I'm nasty after that!'

'Help the Children' had a charity shop in the middle of
the town, and at nine o'clock Jason was outside the door.
There were two women in the shop.

'Good morning,' said the older woman. 'Can we help
you? Are you looking for some cheap clothes?'

'No,' said Jason. 'I want to give you some money.'

'That's nice of you,' said the younger woman.

'Yes,' Jason said. 'I want to give five hundred thousand
pounds to "Help the Children".'

'Five hundred pounds?' said the older woman. 'That's
wonderful!'

'No, no,' said Jason. 'Not five *hundred* pounds. Five
hundred *thousand* pounds!'

The younger woman looked at him. 'Have you *got* five
hundred thousand pounds?'

'Of course I have!' said Jason. 'Well, I haven't got the money now. It's at the court. But I want you to have it.'

The older woman looked at the younger woman, and then at Jason. 'You haven't got any money. Go away.'

'Yes, I have! I won the lottery!' said Jason. 'OK. Listen. Let's say a million pounds. How about that? One million pounds for "Help the Children"!'

The younger woman opened the door, and the older woman said, 'Go away! We don't want you here.'

On Thursday afternoon, Edwin Jones was in the office of Sunshine Lotteries with Mr David Ray. He told Mr Ray the story of Emma Carter and her winning numbers.

'Look, Mr Jones,' said Mr Ray. 'Mr Williams had the winning ticket, so we gave him a cheque for the money. I'm sorry, but I can't help you, or Mrs Carter.'

'But it wasn't Williams's ticket. It was Mrs Carter's.'

'You can't prove that, Mr Jones. All lottery tickets look the same. They don't have names on them.'

'I *can* prove it,' said Edwin Jones. 'Listen. Mrs Carter's ticket is different. You see, she always gets the same numbers. And every week she puts an X on her ticket.'

He told Mr Ray about Mrs Carter's son in Australia. Then he took a lottery ticket out of his pocket. 'This is an old ticket. Look – Mrs Carter always puts an X, *here* . . .

Please go and look at the winning ticket. Now!'

Mr Ray went away and came back five minutes later.
His face was unhappy.

'Well?' said Edwin Jones.

'I don't know,' Mr Ray said 'All the tickets go through
the computer many times, so it's difficult to see—'

'Go away! We don't want you here,' she said.

33

'Mr Ray, is there an X on that ticket, or isn't there?'

Mr Ray looked angrily at Edwin Jones. 'Perhaps there is, and perhaps there isn't,' he said. 'But what does an X prove? Perhaps hundreds of people write an X on their lottery ticket. Perhaps it's Mrs Carter's X, but how do we know? Tell me that, Mr Jones.'

'I can't tell you, but the police can. Now, Mr Ray, please call your bank and stop that cheque. Next, give that lottery ticket to the police. They're going to want it.'

Mr Ray looked unhappy. 'Yes, all right,' he said.

'Then you need a lawyer,' said Mr Jones. 'Because Mrs Carter wants her money – and she wants it now!'

On Thursday afternoon, Jason Williams went to Sally Cash's office and told her about 'Help the Children' and the women in the shop. Sally looked tired.

'Jason, Jason!' she said. 'What *is* all this? I don't want to listen to more lies.'

'I'm telling the truth! I went into the "Help the Children" shop, and they didn't believe me. They said, "You haven't got any money. Go away!" Please telephone them, Miss Cash. I want to give them one million pounds. Please tell them that.'

'But . . .' said Sally Cash. 'But your lottery cheque is at the court . . .'

'All those little children in Africa and India –
I want to help them.'

'Yes, I know. But when I get the money, I want to give
one million pounds to "Help the Children". I thought about
it very carefully. I won all this money in the lottery, and I
want to do something good with it. All those little children
in Africa and India – I want to help them.'

Sally looked at him for a minute.

'Please,' said Jason. 'Please help me. You wanted to help me. You told me that.'

'OK,' Sally said suddenly. 'I believe you. You want to give away a million pounds.' She thought for a second. 'Write a letter to "Help the Children". Write it here, now. Tell them about the million pounds, and put your name on the letter. I'm going to put my name on the letter too, and take the letter to the charity's office now. OK?'

Chapter 7

So who's going to win?

On Thursday evening Sally Cash went home. When she arrived, her husband Colin was in the living-room.

'Hi,' Colin said. 'Did you have a good day?'

'Not bad,' Sally said. 'I'm working on a very interesting case. It's going to be on the news tonight, I think. Let's put the television on.'

After about ten minutes, the newsreader said:

'And now for some news about Sunshine Lotteries. The winner of last Saturday's lottery was Jason Williams. He had the winning ticket, and Sunshine Lotteries gave him a cheque for five million pounds. Now Mr Williams wants to give one million pounds to the charity "Help the Children".

But is it Mr Williams's money? Mrs Emma Carter says that it isn't. This is Mrs Carter's story. In the town last Saturday afternoon a young man hit her on the head and snatched her bag. And in that bag was a lottery ticket — the ticket with the winning numbers. Mrs Carter remembers the numbers very well, she says. So is it Jason Williams's ticket, or

Mrs Carter's ticket? Who's going to get the money?
We have a lawyer with us here, so let's ask him that
question.'

The lawyer talked very interestingly.

'Who's that?' asked Colin.

'That's old Sam Green,' said Sally. 'He's a good lawyer.
He's working for Sunshine Lotteries, I think.'

'And who are you working for, Sally?'

'Jason Williams.'

'And he snatched this woman's bag, yes?' said Colin. 'Is
he going to go to prison, do you think?'

'Perhaps,' Sally said. 'But when he comes out, he's going
to have five million pounds – or four million pounds.'

'But it's Emma Carter's money!' Colin said. 'It was *her*
ticket, in her bag. Of course it was!'

'Well, she *says* it was,' said Sally. 'But how do we know?
She's an old woman. Old people forget things easily.
Perhaps she thought about her lottery numbers, but forgot
to buy a ticket that day.'

'So the bag-snatcher wins, eh?' said Colin. He looked at
Sally. 'He hits an old woman on the head, and wins five
million pounds. Wonderful!'

'I know,' Sally said. 'It's difficult to like Jason Williams,
it's true. He has a wife and child, but his wife left him
because he hit her and the baby. But we must be careful.

Perhaps he *is* telling the truth about the lottery ticket.'

'Never!' said Colin. 'When the case comes to court, they're going to believe Mrs Carter, not Jason Williams. He's nasty!'

'No, he isn't. He wants to give one million pounds to "Help the Children". People are going to like that. What a nice young man!'

'When the case comes to court, they're going to believe Mrs Carter, not Jason Williams.'

Colin laughed. 'Lawyers!' he said. 'So who's going to win, Sally?' he asked.

'The lawyers, of course. Five million pounds is a lot of money, and we're going to have a wonderful time. There's a lot of us, you see. There's Mrs Carter's lawyer, Jason's wife's lawyer, the lawyer for "Help the Children", the lawyer for Sunshine Lotteries – and me, Jason's lawyer. We're going to talk about it in court for days and days. And lawyers are expensive. When we finish, a lot of that five million pounds is going to be *our* money!'

Sally smiled, happily. 'Colin, shall we get a new car? A Mercedes, perhaps?'

GLOSSARY

bank a building or business for keeping money safely

believe to think that something is true or right

buy (past tense **bought**) to get something for money

case a question for a court of law to decide

cell a small room in a prison or police station

champagne an expensive drink

charity help or money for people who are poor or ill

charity shop people give old clothes, books, etc. to charity
    shops; the shops sell the things and give the money to help
    other people

check to look to see if something is all right

cheque a special piece of paper which tells a bank to pay
    money to somebody

clothes shirts, trousers, dresses, coats, etc.

court a place where judges and lawyers decide about law cases

difficult not easy to do or understand

fall (past tense **fell**) to go down suddenly to a lower place; to
    drop

kind *(adj)* good to other people; friendly

kiss *(v)* to touch with the mouth in a loving or friendly way

kiss *(n)* a loving or friendly touch with the mouth

lawyer a person who helps people with the law and talks for
    them in court

lie *(n)* something you say or write which is not true

lottery in a lottery people buy numbered tickets, and every
    week or month some of the tickets win a lot of money

nasty not nice, kind or good

41

news   the story of things which happened yesterday or which are happening now

newspaper   sheets of paper with news, which you can buy every day or every week

pay   to give money for

policeman   somebody whose job is to stop people breaking the law, and to catch people who steal, murder, break into houses, etc.

police station   the office where policemen work

prison   a building for criminals, where the doors are locked

prove   to show that something is right or true

reporter   someone who works for a newspaper, radio or television and tells about things which have happened

send (past tense **sent**)   to make something or someone go somewhere

snatch   to take something in a very quick, violent way

steal (past tense **stole**)   to take something which is not yours

trouble   difficult or worrying times; problems

truth   what is true

unhappy   not happy

win *(v)*   to be the first, or the best, in a game, race, lottery, etc.

winner   a person who wins

The Lottery Winner

ACTIVITIES

Before Reading

1 The title of the story is *The Lottery Winner*. Answer these questions.

1 Is there a lottery in your country?

2 Do you sometimes buy a lottery ticket?

3 Do you know a lottery winner?

4 Is a lottery winner usually a happy person?

2 Read the back cover of the book. How much do you know now about the story? Complete these sentences.

1 Emma Carter is . . .

   a) a young woman.

   b) an old woman.

   c) an old man.

2 Emma buys a lottery ticket . . .

   a) every week.

   b) every month.

   c) every day.

3 Emma has got . . .

   a) no money.

   b) only a little money.

   c) lots of money.

4 Jason Williams . . .

   a) helps old women.

   b) kills old women.

   c) steals money from old women.

3 Read the story introduction on the first page of the book, then answer these questions. Tick one box for each sentence.

	YES	NO
1 Jason has got a winning lottery ticket.	☐	☐
2 Jason's mother and father want his money.	☐	☐
3 Jason is married.	☐	☐
4 Emma is in trouble with the police.	☐	☐
5 Emma is happy.	☐	☐
6 Emma has got a lawyer.	☐	☐

4 What is going to happen in the story? Can you guess? Tick one box for each sentence.

	YES	NO
1 Jason is going to get five million pounds.	☐	☐
2 Emma is going to get five million pounds.	☐	☐
3 Jason is going to go to prison.	☐	☐
4 Emma is going to go to Australia.	☐	☐

While Reading

Read Chapters 1 and 2, then answer these questions.

Who

1 . . . bought some new shoes?
2 . . . hit Emma and took her bag?
3 . . . looked at Emma's head and back when she was in hospital?
4 . . . bought a lottery ticket with the numbers 5, 12, 23, 24, 38, 41?
5 . . . lived with his mother and father?
6 . . . had a lottery ticket with six winning numbers?
7 . . . lived in Australia?
8 . . . brought Emma's shoes and bag to the hospital?
9 . . . found Emma's shoes and bag in the street?

Read Chapter 3, then answer these questions.

Where was Jason . . .

1 at ten o'clock on Monday night?
2 on Tuesday morning?
3 on Tuesday afternoon?
4 on Tuesday night?

Read Chapter 4, then answer these questions.

Why

1 . . . is Jason going to give his mother and father
  £30,000?

2 . . . can't Jason give his parents the money now?

3 . . . did Jason's wife leave him?

4 . . . did Jason's wife come to the police station?

5 . . . did Jason want to hit Sally Cash?

Read Chapters 5 and 6. Here are some untrue sentences about them. Change them into true sentences.

1 Emma telephoned her son in Australia.

2 Emma didn't go to see a lawyer.

3 Emma put her name on her lottery ticket.

4 The women in the charity shop believed Jason.

5 Mr Ray was happy when he heard Emma's story.

6 Sally Cash told Jason to telephone 'Help the Children'.

Before you read Chapter 7, think about the chapter title, *So who's going to win?* Who is going to win? Can you guess?

Read Chapter 7, then answer these questions.

1 How many lawyers are working on the lottery ticket
  case?

2 Why are they going to get a lot of money?

After Reading

1 Why did Emma always choose the same numbers for her lottery ticket? Why were they important to her?

5, 12, 23 _____
24, 38 _____
41 _____

2 What happens after the end of the story? You choose. Tick one box for each sentence. Then use some of the sentences to write a paragraph. Join your sentences with *and, but* or *so* where possible.

	YES	NO
1 Emma gets a lot of money.	☐	☐
2 Emma goes to Australia to see her son.	☐	☐
3 Emma gives one million pounds to 'Help the Children'.	☐	☐
4 Jason gets a lot of money.	☐	☐
5 Jason's wife gets half of his money.	☐	☐
6 Jason gives one million pounds to 'Help the Children'.	☐	☐
7 Jason gives £30,000 each to his mother and father.	☐	☐
8 Jason goes to prison.	☐	☐
9 Sally and her husband buy a new car.	☐	☐

3 Here is a new illustration for the story. Find the best place in the story to put the picture, and answer these questions.

The picture goes on page _____.

1 Who is on television? Why?
2 Who is watching television?
3 What is she going to do next? Why?

Now write a caption for the illustration.

Caption: _____

4 **When Emma saw Jason on television, she telephoned the police. Write out the conversation in the correct order and put in the speakers' names. Emma speaks first (5).**

1 _____ 'Are you sure it's the same man?'

2 _____ 'Because of the numbers. I always choose the same numbers.'

3 _____ 'Can I help you, madam?'

4 _____ 'Because he's got this week's winning lottery ticket.'

5 _____ 'Hullo – police?'

6 _____ 'How do you know that it's your ticket?'

7 _____ 'I see. Well, I'm going to send a policeman to talk to you, Mrs Carter.'

8 _____ 'My name's Mrs Emma Carter. A young man stole my handbag on Saturday. I can see him on television now.'

9 _____ 'Thank you very much.'

10 _____ 'Why is he on television, madam?'

11 _____ 'Yes, I'm sure. And he's got my lottery ticket.'

5 **Imagine that you are Jason. Use these words to complete his letter to 'Help the Children'. (Use each word once.)**

children, going, is, lawyer, letter, lottery, one, pounds, to, won, write

Dear Sir/Madam

My name _____ Jason Williams. I _____ five million _____ in the _____. I want _____ help poor _____, so I am _____ to give you _____ million pounds. My _____ believes me, and she is going to _____ her name on this _____ too.

Yours faithfully

Jason Williams

6 **Put these words into two groups.**

nice, kind, nasty, happy, unhappy, angry, wonderful

good _____

bad _____

Now write sentences like this about these characters.

Jason Williams is nasty because he stole Emma Carter's bag.

Jason Williams	Sally Cash
Simon Carter	Lily Williams
Fiona Williams	Emma Carter

7 **Imagine that you win five million pounds in the lottery. What are you going to do with it? Write five sentences. Use some of these verbs.**

buy, give, go, stop, live

ABOUT THE AUTHOR

Rosemary Border is a very experienced teacher and writer, who has also worked as an editor, a lawyer, and a journalist. She is the author of a great number of books for learners of English – more than she can remember. 'I stopped counting after 150,' she says. She has written or retold more than 80 graded readers, including several stories for the Oxford Bookworms Library. Among these are *The Piano* (an original story, at Stage 2) and *Tooth and Claw* (a collection of short stories by Saki, at Stage 3). She lives and works in Suffolk, in the east of England.

OXFORD BOOKWORMS LIBRARY

Classics • Crime & Mystery • Factfiles • Fantasy & Horror
Human Interest • Playscripts • Thriller & Adventure
True Stories • World Stories

The OXFORD BOOKWORMS LIBRARY provides enjoyable reading in English, with a wide range of classic and modern fiction, non-fiction, and plays. It includes original and adapted texts in seven carefully graded language stages, which take learners from beginner to advanced level. An overview is given on the next pages.

All Stage 1 titles are available as audio recordings, as well as over eighty other titles from Starter to Stage 6. All Starters and many titles at Stages 1 to 4 are specially recommended for younger learners. Every Bookworm is illustrated, and Starters and Factfiles have full-colour illustrations.

The OXFORD BOOKWORMS LIBRARY also offers extensive support. Each book contains an introduction to the story, notes about the author, a glossary, and activities. Additional resources include tests and worksheets, and answers for these and for the activities in the books. There is advice on running a class library, using audio recordings, and the many ways of using Oxford Bookworms in reading programmes. Resource materials are available on the website <www.oup.com/bookworms>.

The *Oxford Bookworms Collection* is a series for advanced learners. It consists of volumes of short stories by well-known authors, both classic and modern. Texts are not abridged or adapted in any way, but carefully selected to be accessible to the advanced student.

You can find details and a full list of titles in the *Oxford Bookworms Library Catalogue* and *Oxford English Language Teaching Catalogues*, and on the website <www.oup.com/bookworms>.

THE OXFORD BOOKWORMS LIBRARY
GRADING AND SAMPLE EXTRACTS

STARTER • 250 HEADWORDS

present simple – present continuous – imperative –
can/cannot, must – going to (future) – simple gerunds …

Her phone is ringing – but where is it?

Sally gets out of bed and looks in her bag. No phone. She looks under the bed. No phone. Then she looks behind the door. There is her phone. Sally picks up her phone and answers it. *Sally's Phone*

STAGE 1 • 400 HEADWORDS

… past simple – coordination with *and, but, or* –
subordination with *before, after, when, because, so* …

I knew him in Persia. He was a famous builder and I worked with him there. For a time I was his friend, but not for long. When he came to Paris, I came after him – I wanted to watch him. He was a very clever, very dangerous man. *The Phantom of the Opera*

STAGE 2 • 700 HEADWORDS

… present perfect – *will* (future) – *(dont) have to, must not, could* –
comparison of adjectives – simple *if* clauses – past continuous –
tag questions – *ask/tell* + infinitive …

While I was writing these words in my diary, I decided what to do. I must try to escape. I shall try to get down the wall outside. The window is high above the ground, but I have to try. I shall take some of the gold with me – if I escape, perhaps it will be helpful later. *Dracula*

STAGE 3 • 1000 HEADWORDS

... should, may – present perfect continuous – *used to* – past perfect –
causative – relative clauses – indirect statements ...

Of course, it was most important that no one should see
Colin, Mary, or Dickon entering the secret garden. So Colin
gave orders to the gardeners that they must all keep away
from that part of the garden in future. *The Secret Garden*

STAGE 4 • 1400 HEADWORDS

... past perfect continuous – passive (simple forms) –
would conditional clauses – indirect questions –
relatives with *where/when* – gerunds after prepositions/phrases ...

I was glad. Now Hyde could not show his face to the world
again. If he did, every honest man in London would be proud
to report him to the police. *Dr Jekyll and Mr Hyde*

STAGE 5 • 1800 HEADWORDS

... future continuous – future perfect –
passive (modals, continuous forms) –
would have conditional clauses – modals + perfect infinitive ...

If he had spoken Estella's name, I would have hit him. I was so
angry with him, and so depressed about my future, that I could
not eat the breakfast. Instead I went straight to the old house.
Great Expectations

STAGE 6 • 2500 HEADWORDS

... passive (infinitives, gerunds) – advanced modal meanings –
clauses of concession, condition

When I stepped up to the piano, I was confident. It was as if I
knew that the prodigy side of me really did exist. And when I
started to play, I was so caught up in how lovely I looked that
I didn't worry how I would sound. *The Joy Luck Club*

Remember Miranda

ROWENA AKINYEMI

Cathy Wilson is driving to Norfolk, to begin her new job with the Harvey family. She is going to look after the two young children, Tim and Susan. Cathy meets the children's father, and their grandmother, and their aunt. She meets Nick, the farmer who lives across the fields. But she doesn't meet Miranda, the children's mother, because Miranda is dead.

She died two years ago, and Cathy cannot learn anything about her. Everybody remembers Miranda, but nobody wants to talk about her . . .

Ned Kelly: A True Story

CHRISTINE LINDOP

When he was a boy, he was poor and hungry. When he was a young man, he was still poor and still hungry. He learnt how to steal horses, he learnt how to fight, he learnt how to live – outside the law. Australia in the 1870s was a hard, wild place. Rich people had land, poor people didn't. So the rich got richer, and the poor stayed poor.

Some say Ned Kelly was a bad man. Some say he was a good man but the law was bad. This is the true story of Australia's most famous outlaw.